CONSERVATORY CANADA™

New Millennium Voice Series

GRADE FOUR

Editorial Committee
D.F. Cook
Elizabeth Parsons
Anita Ruthig

With thanks to Lisa Martin, Jennifer Floris, and Debra Wanless for their assistance.

Official Examination Repertoire List Pieces and Studies of Conservatory Canada - Grade 4

*Publication of the New Millennium Voice Series is made possible
by a generous grant from Dr. Don Wright.*

© 1999 Conservatory Canada
Published and Distributed by Novus Via Music Group Inc.
All Rights Reserved.

ISBN 978-0-88909-193-1

Novus Via Music Group Inc.
189 Douglas Street, Stratford, Ontario, Canada N5A 5P8
(519) 273-7520   www.NVmusicgroup.com

cover design:
Robin E. Cook, AOCA

About the Series

The *New Millennium Voice Series* is the official repertoire for Conservatory Canada examinations. This graded series, in eight volumes (Grade 1 to Grade 8), is designed not only to serve the needs of teachers and students for examinations, but it is also a valuable teaching resource and comprehensive anthology for any singer. The List Pieces have been carefully selected and edited, and represent repertoire from the Baroque, Classical, Romantic/Impressionist, and 20th-century periods. In addition, each volume includes the syllabus requirements for the grade, a graded arrangement of *O Canada* (with words in English and French), and a Glossary containing a short biography of each composer. Conservatory Canada requires that at least one Canadian composition be performed in every examination. Composers working in Canada are well represented in the series. A small asterisk next to their name identifies them. Photographs of some Canadian composers are included with the biography.

Notes on Editing

Most composers in the Baroque and Classical periods included only sparse dynamic, articulation, tempo and other performance indications in their scores. Where we felt it necessary, we have added suggested markings. The *New Millennium Series* is not an Urtext edition. All editorial markings are intended to be helpful suggestions rather than a final authority. The choice of tempo is a matter of personal taste, technical ability, and appropriateness of style. Most of our suggested metronome markings are expressed within a range of tempi. In the 19th and 20th centuries, composers included more performance indications in their scores, and as a consequence, fewer editorial markings have been required.

No markings have been used to suggest phrasing and breathing. In accordance with Conservatory Canada's policy regarding redundant accidentals, we have followed the practice that a barline cancels accidentals. Unnecessary accidentals following the barline have been used only in exceptional circumstances.

Bearing in mind acceptable performance practices, you are free to use your own judgement, musicianship and imagination in changing any editorial marking, especially in the areas of dynamics, articulation, and phrasing.

Every effort has been made to identify the authorship of texts and translations. Where we have not been able to confirm that the authorship is generally accepted as being anonymous, we have used the term "unknown".

The pieces in the *New Millennium Series* have been chosen as an introduction to enjoyable repertoire that is fun to sing while, at the same time, helps to develop your technique and musicianship. We hope you will explore the broad variety of styles and periods represented in this book. It is important that you learn as many pieces as possible before deciding which ones you will sing in the examination.

London, Ontario
September 1999

The Conservatory Canada Voice Syllabus gives full details regarding examinations. Teachers, students, and parents are advised to consult the most recent Syllabus for current requirements, regulations, procedures and deadline for application.

GRADE 4 - Table of Contents

LIST A

LIST B

*Indicates Canadian Composer

CRADLE SONG

Petite Berceuse, Op. 59, No. 5

Anonymous

Antony Arensky
(1861-1906)

Sleep,   my dar - ling
Dors,   n'aie pas peur,

have   no   fear,   for   thy   Mo - ther_ watch - es   near.
mon   en - fant,   Car   ta   mè - re   sur   toi   se   penche,

sun - light dies. All the night the faith - ful breeze
loin s'en - fuit. *La bri - se tou - te la nuit.*

mur - mur'd low a - mong the trees._____
Mur - mure à tra - vers les branches._____

"Lit - tle breeze, now tell me, pray,
Dou - ce bri - se, je vous prie,

MARIENWÜRMCHEN
Ladybug

Des Knaben Wunderhorn
English version by Roberta Stephen

Johannes Brahms
(1833-1897)

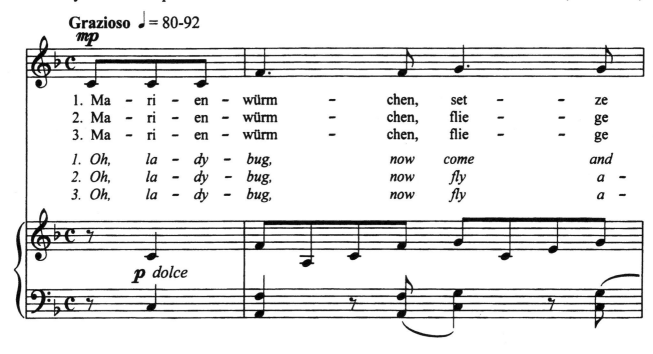

1. Ma – ri – en – würm – chen, set – – ze dich, auf mein – e Hand_____ auf mein – e
2. Ma – ri – en – würm – chen, flie – – ge weg, dein Häus – chen brennt,_____ die Kin – der
3. Ma – ri – en – würm – chen, flie – – ge weg, zu Nach – bars Kind,_____ zu Nach – bars

1. *Oh, la – dy – bug,* now come and stand up – on my hand,_____ up – on my
2. *Oh, la – dy – bug,* now fly a – way, your house it burns._____ Your child – ren
3. *Oh, la – dy – bug,* now fly a – way, to oth – er friends,_____ to oth – er

7

4

Hand,___ ich tu dir nichts zu leid - e es soll dir
schrein__ so seh - re, ach, so seh - re; die Bö - se
Kind,___ sie tun dir nichts zu Lei - de; es soll dir

hand.___ For I will nev - er harm you. No harm to
cry___ Your child - ren cry so sad - ly The ev - il
friends.___ For they will nev - er harm you. They on - ly

7

nichts zu Leid ge - schehn, will nur
Spin - ne spinnt sie ein, Mari - en
ja kein Leid ge - schehn, sie wolln

you will ev - er come. On - ly
spid - er spins her web. La - dy -
want to see your wings pret - ty

SHENANDOAH

Traditional (United States)

American Folksong
arr. Steven Fielder

leave you, A - way,_____ you roll - ing riv - er. Oh

Shen - an - doah,_____ I'll not de - ceive you. A - way,_____ I'm bound a -

way, 'Cross the wide Mis - sou - ri._____

FAREWELL TO NOVA SCOTIA

Traditional (Nova Scotia)

*Canadian Folksong
arr. D.F. Cook

Sadly ♩ = 80-92

1. The___ sun was___ set-ting___
grieve to___ leave my___

in the___ West, The___ birds were sing-ing on ev'-ry___ tree,___
na - tive___ land, I___ grieve to leave my___ com - rades___ all,___

All___ na - ture seem'd in - clined for___ rest, But___
And my pa - rents whom I___ held so___ dear, And the

13

ev – er heave a sigh__ and a wish for me?

wish for me?

2. The__ drums they do beat and the

wars do a – larm. The__ cap – tain calls, we must o – bey,__

So fare-well, fare-well to__ No - va Sco - tia's charms, For it's

ear - ly in the morn - ing I am far, far a - way.__ Fare -

well to No - va Sco - tia, the sea - bound__ coast! Let your moun - tains dark and

drear - y____ be, For when I am far a - way on the

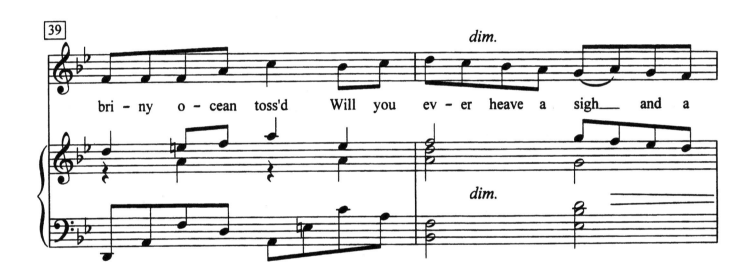

bri - ny o - cean toss'd Will you ev - er heave a sigh____ and a

wish for me?____ 3. I

D.S. al Fine

THE OLD "MAYFLOWER"

Traditional (Newfoundland)

*Canadian Folksong
arr. D.F. Cook

old tin pan. Da da da da dot did - dle la, da da did - dle la did - dle

la da da, did - dle la did - dle la dot did - dle did - dle la de did - dle la did - dle la da

day. Out with the car - go___ dry___ fish and ale,___ Old Don___ Mills he

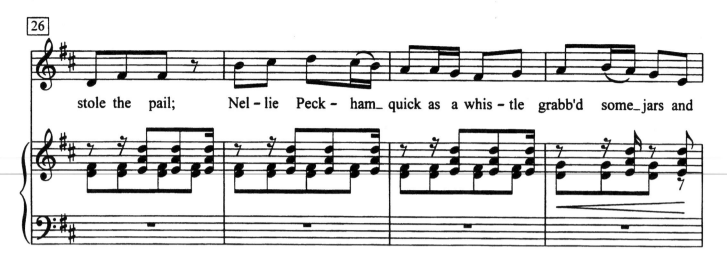

26

stole the pail; Nel - lie Peck - ham_ quick as a whis - tle grabb'd some_ jars and

30

stole the ket - tle. Cook - ie_ Gil - lis,_ the_ sec - ond man,_

fz *mp staccato*

35

poco rit. *ten.* *ten.*

Car - ried the wood a - cross Cape Sand; He piled it up like an old church_tow'r, And

legato *poco rit.*

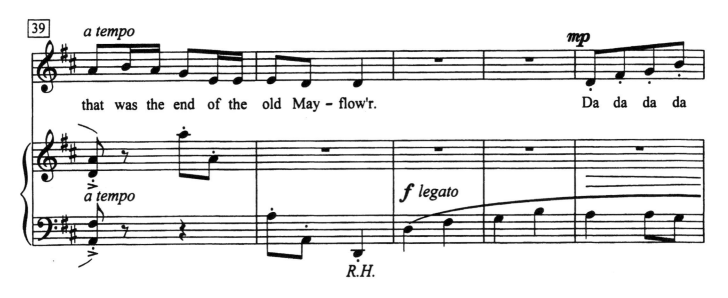

that was the end of the old May – flow'r.   Da   da   da   da

dot did – dle la da   da did – dle la did – dle la da   da, did – dle la did – dle la dot

did – dle did – dle la de did – dle la did – dle la da,   la did – dle la da   day.___

ONE MORNING IN THE MEADOW

Traditional (Germany)

German Folksong
arr. D.F. Cook

1. One
2. When

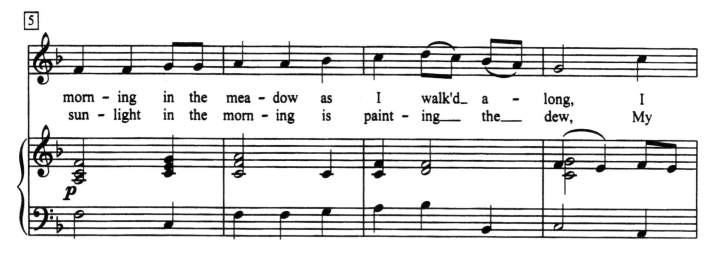

morn - ing in the mea - dow as I walk'd a - long, I
sun - light in the morn - ing is paint - ing the dew, My

heard a young mai - den a - sing - ing this song.
song up - ward soar - ing till it's lost in the blue.

I KNOW WHERE I'M GOIN'

Traditional

Irish Folksong
arr. H. Hughes

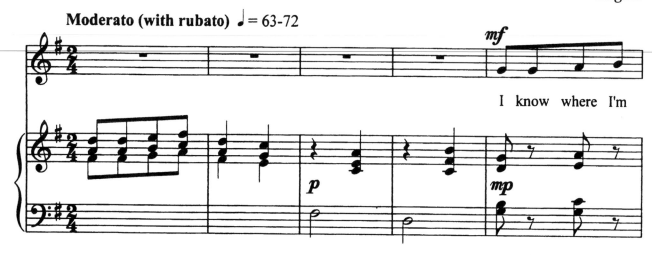

Shoes of fine green lea – ther, Combs to buc – kle my hair, And a ring for ev – 'ry

fin – ger. Some say he's black,* But

I say he's bon – ny, The fair – est of them all My__ hand – some, win – some

*Black: dour, ungracious

25

John - ny. Fea - ther beds are soft, And

paint - ed rooms are bon - ny, But I would leave them all To___

go with my love John - ny.

I know where I'm go - in', And I know who's go - in'

with me, I know who I love,_____ But the dear knows who I'll

mar - ry!

WIDMUNG
Dedication, Op. 14, No. 1

Anonymous

Robert Franz
(1815-1892)

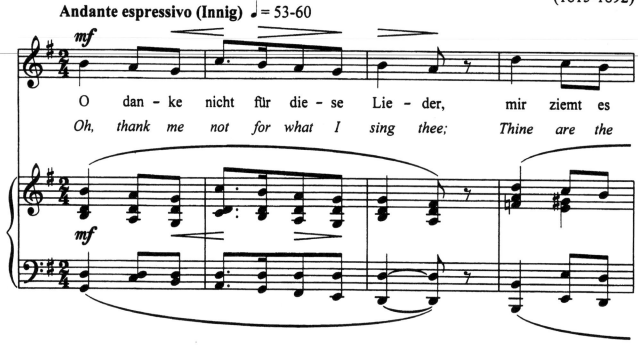

Andante espressivo (Innig) ♩ = 53-60

O dan - ke nicht für die - se Lie - der, mir ziemt es
Oh, thank me not for what I sing thee; Thine are the

dank - bar Dir zu sein; Du gabst sie mir,___ ich ge - be
songs, no gift of mine. Thou gav'st them me;___ I but re-

28

COME, SEE WHERE
GOLDEN-HEARTED SPRING
Menuet from *Berenice*

Clifford Bax

Georg Frederick Händel
(1685-1759)

16 *mf*

sun. Hark, hark birds now, all in the green – wood_ ways,

21

Pipe songs, mer – ry, mer – ry round – e – lays, With

25 *poco dim.*

sun – ny hours by day_____ And a clear moon by night,_____ What_

IT WAS A LOVER AND HIS LASS

William Shakespeare

Thomas Morley
(1557-1602)
arr. J.M. Diack

spring time, in spring time, in spring time, The on - ly pret - ty

ring time, When birds do sing, hey ding a ding a ding, hey

ding a ding a ding, hey ding a ding a ding; Sweet lov - ers love the spring.

THE BUTTERFLY AND THE SHADOW

Margaret Rose

Stuart Young
(20th Century)

day I was so hap-py: I saw a but-ter-fly,____ And a

shad-ow where a gold-en sun On a gras-sy hill did lie.____

36

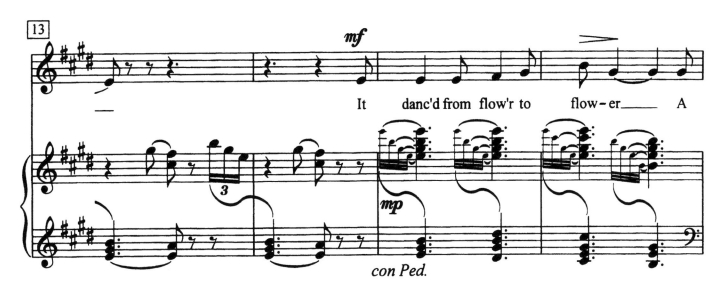

It danc'd from flow'r to flow-er___ A

- cross the sun - lit hill,___ Till the shad - ow fell a - cross the flow - ers And

hush'd them soft and still.___ But

some-how I grew lone - ly: The shad-ow turn'd to grey._____ The but-ter-fly took

wing a-gain, And soft-ly flew a-way._____ And

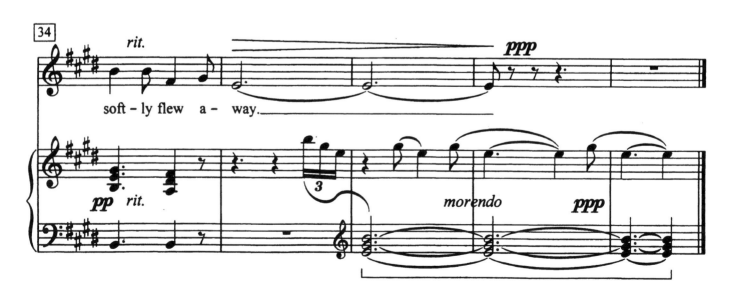

soft-ly flew a-way._____

SLEEP LITTLE JESUS
(A Cradle Carol)

Noreen Moore

*W.H. Anderson
(1882-1955)

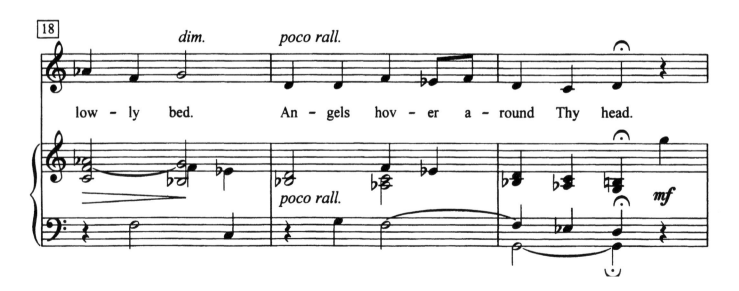

Sleep, lit – tle Je – sus, sleep to – night.

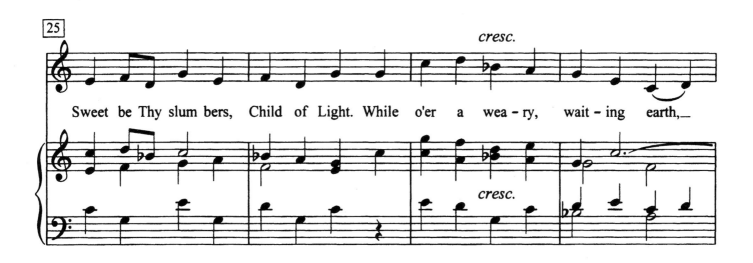

Sweet be Thy slum bers, Child of Light. While o'er a wea – ry, wait – ing earth,__

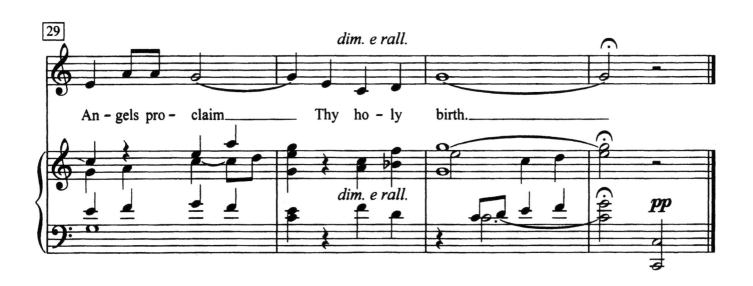

An – gels pro – claim_____ Thy ho – ly birth._____

TWILIGHT LULLABY

Amy Dooley

Thomas F. Dunhill
(1877-1946)

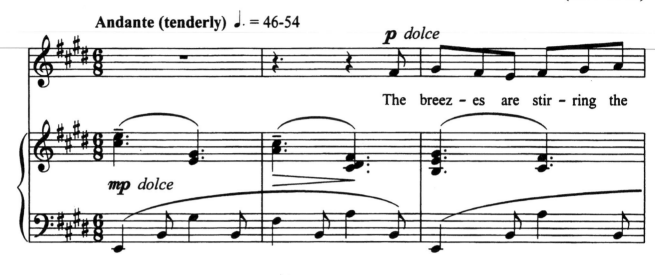

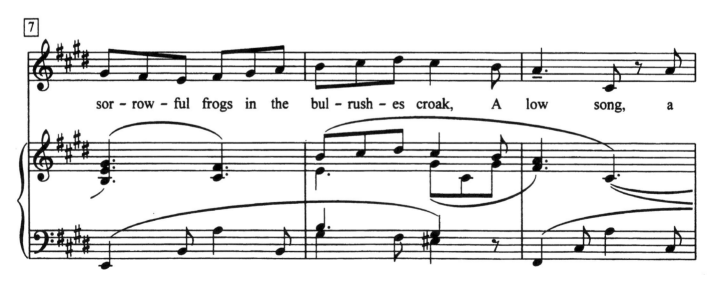

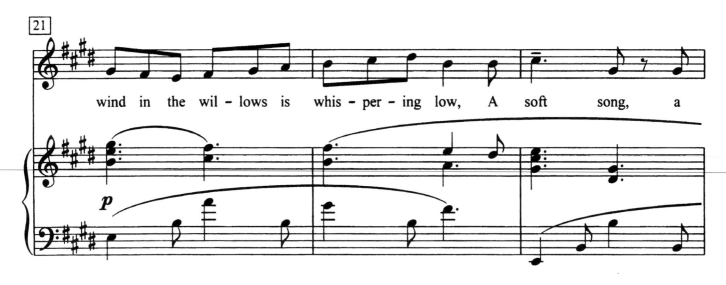

wind in the wil - lows is whis - per - ing low, A soft song, a

sweet song; The jar of a night owl gives warn - ing of woe, A

wild song, a weird song. Rust - ling a dor - mouse comes

forth from his nest, The mu – sic of twi – light says, "Hush thee and rest"_____

And so the world sleeps._____

IT'S RAINING

from *Five of 5*

Margaret Fleming

*Robert Fleming
(1921-1976)

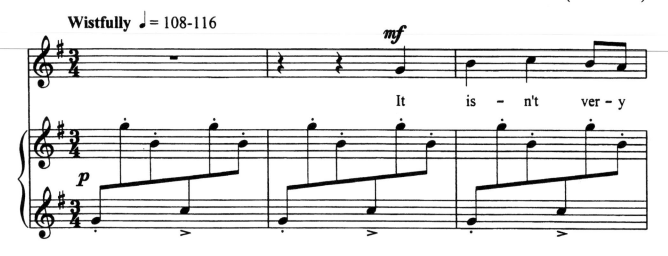

It is-n't ver-y

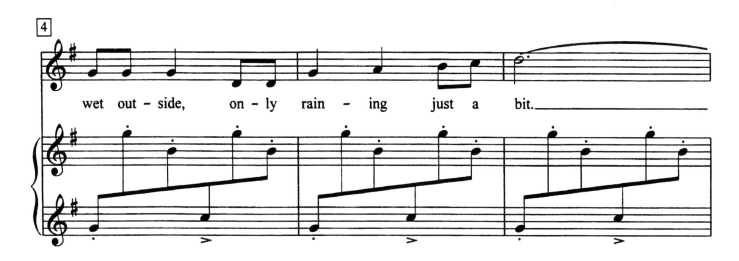

wet out-side, on-ly rain-ing just a bit.___

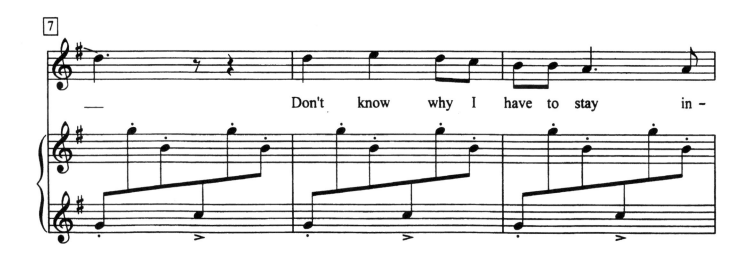

Don't know why I have to stay in-

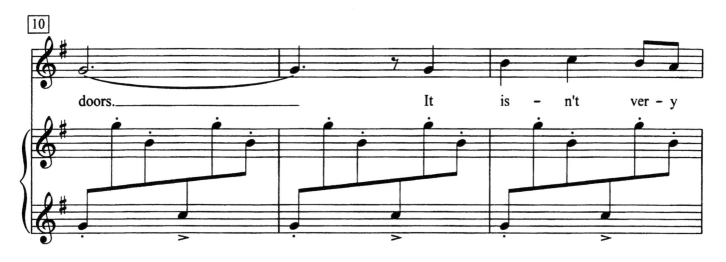

doors._____ It is - n't ver - y

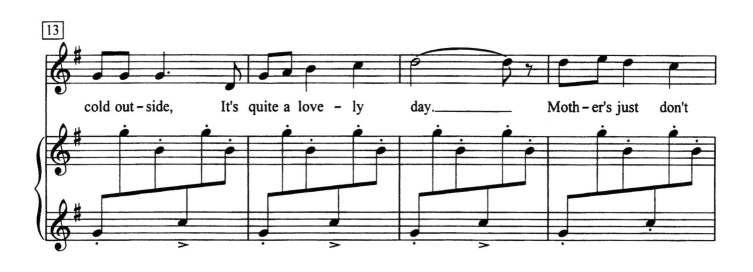

cold out - side, It's quite a love - ly day._____ Moth - er's just don't

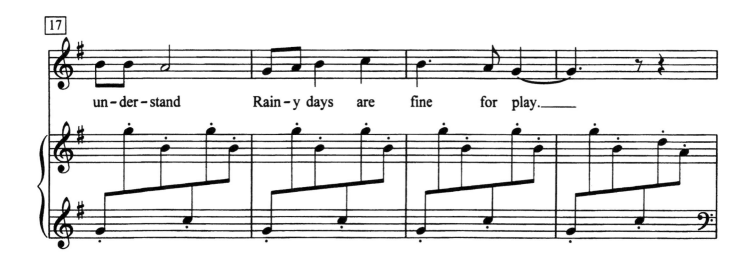

un - der - stand Rain - y days are fine for play.____

And when   I grow up   so big and tall, As

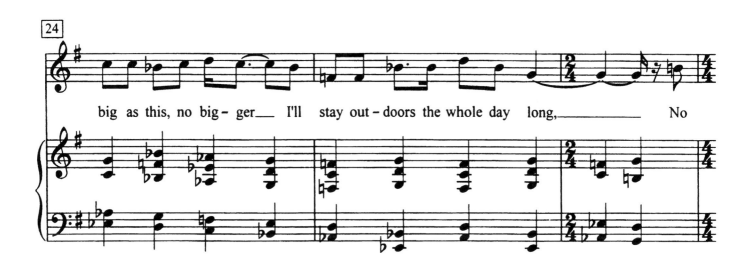

big   as this, no big - ger___   I'll   stay out - doors the whole day   long,_____   No

mat - ter   what   the weath - er._____

48

THE DREAM PEDLAR

Margaret Rose

John Longmire
(1902-   )

Down the hill he

takes his way When the winds come out   to play;   Hear him whist – ling

shrill and deep When the great big world's a - sleep._____

49

Come, my chil – dren, come and buy Ai – ry fai – ry wings and

fly,_____ Ride a ti – ny sil – ver star See the

world and tra – vel far._____ Quick! the ped – dlar

can-not stay, Up the hill he goes his way,_____ Whist - ling in the

poco rit. *mf*

mis - ty gloom_____ Ov - er the rim, the rim__ of the

poco rit.

mf

a tempo

moon._____

a tempo

THE TIGER

Peter Jenkyns

Peter Jenkyns
(1921-   )

Mysteriously ♩ = 100-116

Prowl – ing round the for – est when the night is dark and wild, Jaws a – gape and eyes a – flame, the foe of man and child; The Ti – ger lurks and hunts a – lone his

© 1956 Elkin & Co.

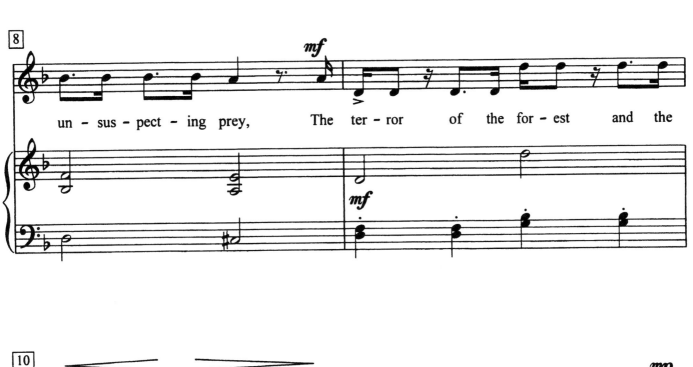

un - sus - pect - ing prey, The ter - ror of the for - est and the

king_____ of night and day._____ Be

ware you ti - mid An - te - lope as at the stream you drink, The

watch - ing eyes are on_____ you, he's near - er than you think; For-

get your thirst and run in time and live to tell the tale Of the

ter - ror of the for - est who was close_____ up - on your

trail._____ He who hunts the Ti - ger and

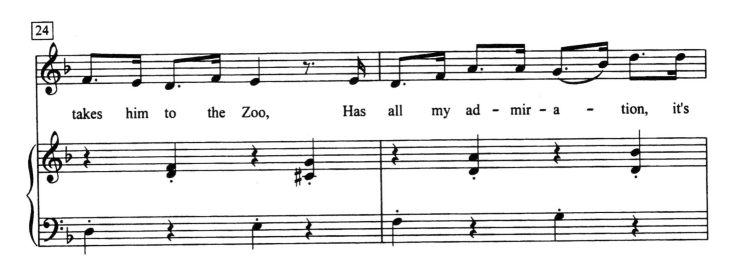

takes him to the Zoo, Has all my ad - mir - a - tion, it's

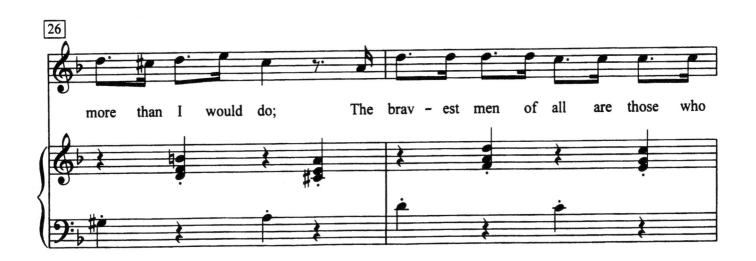

more than I would do; The brav - est men of all are those who

crouch be - neath the stars For the ter - ror of the for - est whom we

see_____ be - hind the bars._____ Now

I am like the An - te - lope, as ti - nmid as can be, And

hunt - ing sav - age ti - gers would nev - er do for me; The

on - ly time I'm fear - less is when I'm ly - ing snug On the

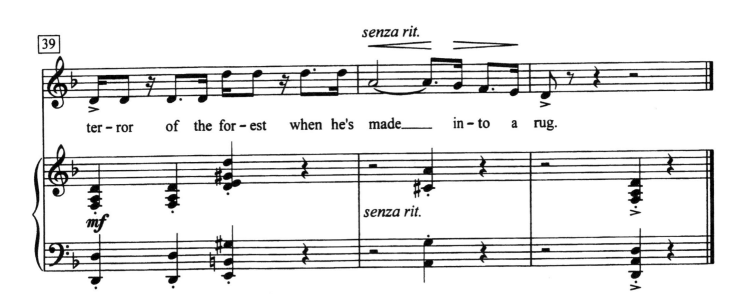

ter - ror of the for - est when he's made____ in - to a rug.

THE SHELL

Margaret G. Rhodes

George Rathbone
(20th Century)

once I found a lit – tle shell_____ Up – on the peb – bled shore, A

thing so won – der – ful and strange Was nev – er mine be –

fore. A mer–maid must have wrought and carv'd So

beau–ti–ful a thing,_____ Pale pink and white and rain–bow–

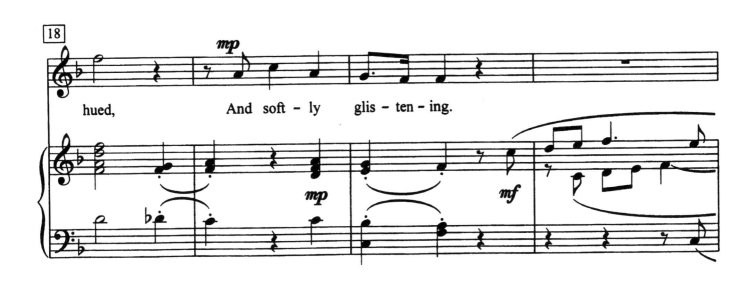

hued, And soft–ly glis–ten–ing.

I press'd the shell a – gainst my

ear,_____ And then it seem'd to me I heard_____ a

haunt – ing, far – off tune From some un – chart – ed sea.

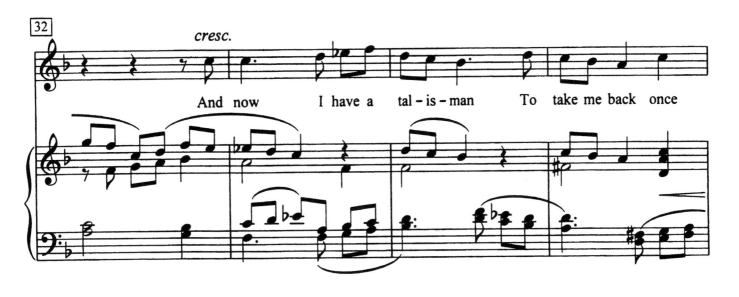

And now I have a tal-is-man To take me back once

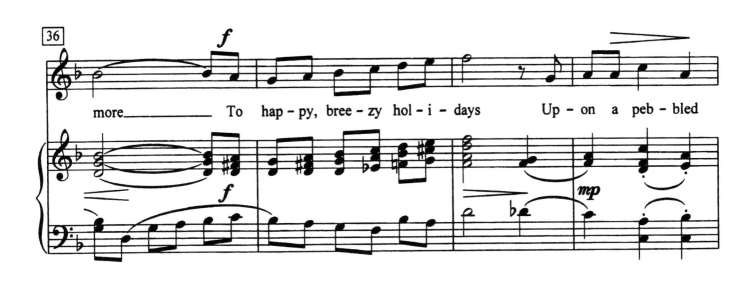

more____ To hap-py, bree-zy hol-i-days Up-on a peb-bled

shore.

IN TWINKLEDOWN VALLEY

Doris Rowley

Alec Rowley
(1892-1958)

an - to - ny Brown, Yet no one has seen him in mea - dow or town.

But out on the moors when the

moon - light is there, He ca - pers and fid - dles his tunes in the air,____

And down peep the stars, while the

rab – bits creep out, To see what this wee danc – ing elf is a – bout.__

He plays till the moon draws a

veil o'er her head, And all the brown bun - nies creep back— to their bed, Then

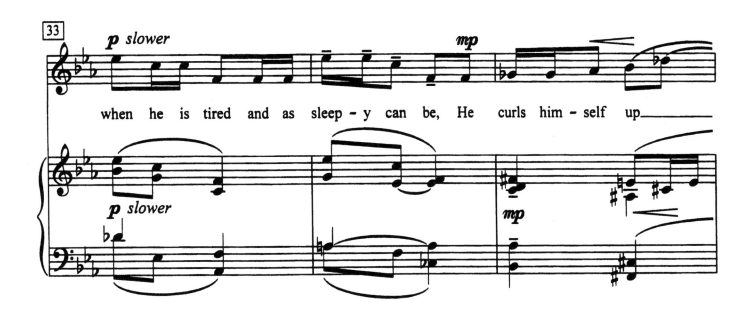

when he is tired and as sleep - y can be, He curls him - self up—

__ 'neath a wild cher - ry tree.

BOATS OF MINE

Robert Louis Stevenson

Anne Stratton Miller
(20th Century)

Dark brown is__ the riv - er, Gold - en is__ the

sand. It flows a - long for ev - er, With

trees on ei - ther hand.   Green leaves_ a -

colla voce

float - ing,   Cas - tles of the foam,

Boats of mine a - boat - ing,   When will all come

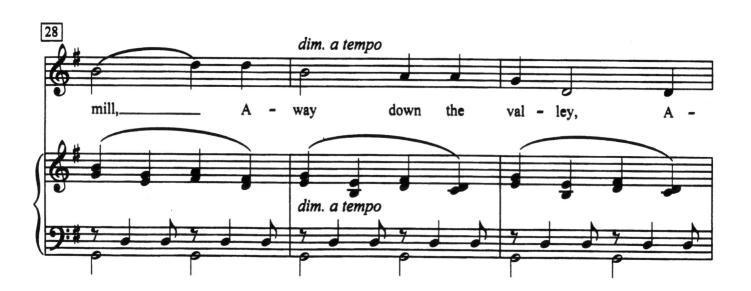

way down the hill. A-

way down the riv - er, A hun - dred miles or

more, Oth - er lit - tle chil - dren Shall

bring my boats a - shore,

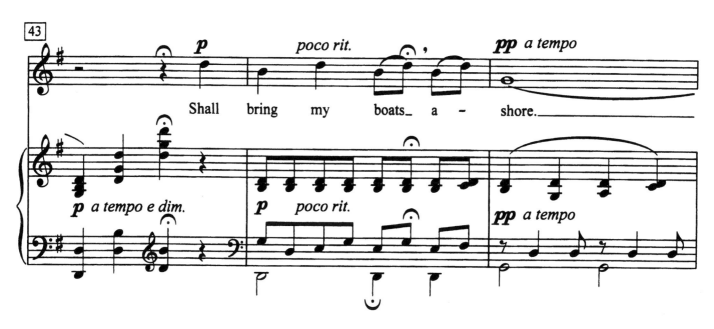

Shall bring my boats a - shore.

THE LAMB

William Blake

Cecil Sharman
(?-1973)

Simply (with much expression) ♩ = 72-84

p

Lit-tle Lamb, who made thee?

Dost thou know who made thee? Gave thee life, and bid thee

feed. By the stream and o'er the mead;

71

Gave thee cloth - ing of de - light,   Soft - est cloth - ing, wool - ly,

bright;   Gave thee such a ten - der voice,____ Mak - ing

all the vales re - joice?____ Lit - tle Lamb, who made thee?

called by His name._____ Lit - tle Lamb, God bless thee! Lit - tle Lamb, God bless thee!

a tempo

THE PATH TO THE MOON

Madeline C. Thomas

Alec Rowley
(1892-1958)

Andantino ♩. = 52-60

mp

mf cantabile

I

long to sail the path to the moon On a deep_ blue night, when the

wind is cool: A glist - 'ning path, that runs out to sea,

Sil - ver the sails to car - ry me, to car - ry, car - ry, car - ry me o - ver the sea.

TIT-WILLOW

from *The Mikado*

William S. Gilbert

Arthur S. Sullivan
(1842-1900)

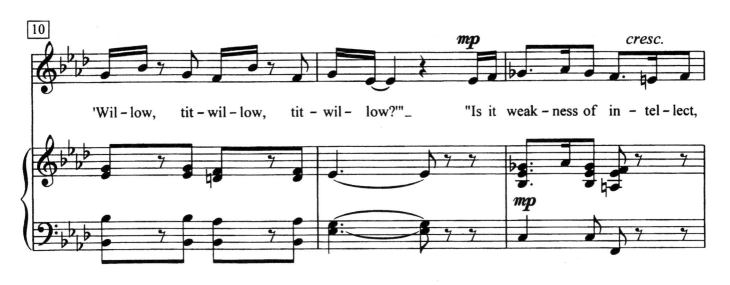

'Wil - low, tit - wil - low, tit - wil - low?'"_ "Is it weak - ness of in - tel - lect,

bir - die?" I cried, "Or a ra - ther tough worm in your lit - tle in - side?" With a

shake of his poor lit - tle head he re - plied, "Oh wil - low, tit - wil - low, tit -

wil – low, tit – wil – low, tit – wil – low!_ He_ sobb'd and he sigh'd, and a

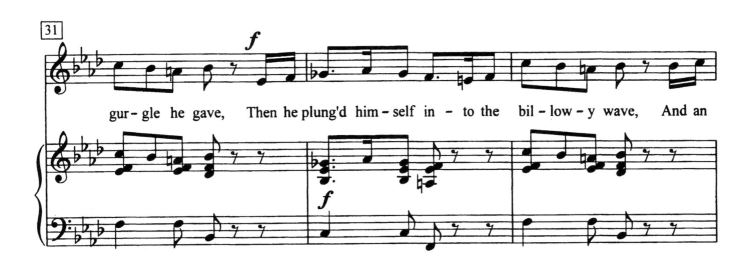

gur – gle he gave, Then he plung'd him – self in – to the bil – low – y wave, And an

e – cho a – rose from the su – i – cide's grave "Oh, wil – low, tit – wil – low, tit –

wil-low,   tit-wil-low,   tit-wil-low!"_   And if   you re-main cal-lous and

ob-du-rate, I   Shall_ per-ish as he   did, and you will know why, Though I

pro-bab-ly shall not ex claim as I die,   "Oh, wil-low, tit-wil-low, tit-wil-low!"

L'ÉTÉ
The Summer

Caroline Tolton

*Ruth Watson Henderson
(1932-   )

Giocoso ♩. = 104-112

Oh! que j'a-

-do - re l'é - té, c'est ma sai - son pré - fé - rée, Et

quand il fait très chaud,_____ Je chan - te, je dan - se, c'est

beau!_____ A-

vec tous mes a - mis On s'a - muse et on rit,_____ On

prend des vers de ter - re, On pê - che dans la ri - viè - re.___

___ Oh! que j'a - do - re l'é - té, C'est ma sai - son pré - fé-

rée Et quand il fait très chaud,___ Je chan - te, je

dan - se, c'est beau!

Je vais au pi - que - ni - que,

J'ai hor - reur des mou - ti - ques; Quand vien - nent les four -

47

mis,_____ Très vi - te je m'en-fuis.   Oh! que j'a-

51

-do - re l'é - té,   c'est ma sai - son   pré - fé -

54

rée,   Et quand il fait très chaud,_____   Je

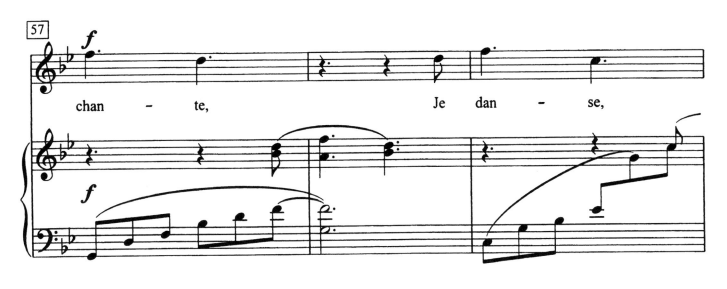

chan - te, Je dan - se,

c'est beau!

THE SUMMER
English translation by D.F. Cook

Oh! I adore summer,
it's my favourite season,
and when I'm very warm,
I sing, I dance, it's wonderful!

With all my friends, we always have fun,
we go to the beach, we fish in the river.

Oh! I adore summer, ...

I go on a picnic,
I hate mosquitos;
when they are swarming
I escape quickly.

Oh! I adore summer, ...

GLOSSARY
Compiled by Debra Wanless

About the Composers in Grade Four

*ANDERSON, William Henry (1882-1955). Canada. Anderson was born in England and studied music in London where he sang in several church choirs and with an opera company. Chronic bronchitis ended his career as a vocal soloist and he decided to seek a less humid climate. He emigrated to Canada in 1910, settling in Winnipeg, Manitoba where he worked as a vocal teacher, choir director and composer. He composed more than 150 songs and approximately 40 church anthems.

ARENSKY, Antony Stepanovich (1861-1906). Russia. Arensky's parents were both musical and they encouraged the development of their son's musical talents. He went on to study composition at the St. Petersburg Conservatory with the famous composer Rimsky-Korsakov. Arensky spent most of his life as a teacher at the Moscow Conservatory and his circle of friends included several of the most important Russian composers of the time such as Balakirev and Tchaikovsky. In his later years (1894-1901), Arensky served as director of the Imperial Chapel in St. Petersburg. He composed operas, a ballet, two symphonies, chamber music, piano works and numerous songs. His music is stylistically quite similar to that of Tchaikovsky, but although it is technically correct, it lacks Tchaikovsky's sparkle and imagination.

BRAHMS, Johannes (1833-1897). Germany. Brahms was the son of a double-bass player who was also his first teacher. Although his parents originally hoped that the young Brahms would become an orchestral player, they soon realized that he was a very gifted pianist. His early performing experiences were limited to playing in taverns and saloons, but a concert tour with the great Hungarian violinist Joachim greatly advanced his career as a pianist. A friend of Schumann and Liszt, Brahms also established himself as a skilled composer. He wrote many songs (called *Lieder* in German) using works by the great German poets, arranged many German folk songs and also composed symphonies and choral works.

*COOK, Donald F. (born 1937). Canada.  Donald Cook grew up and received his early musical training in St. John's, Newfoundland. After further studies in New York City and London, England, Dr. Cook returned to Newfoundland to become the founding director of the School of Music at Memorial University. Since 1992, he has served as Principal of Western Ontario Conservatory (now Conservatory Canada). Most of Dr. Cook's compositions are for solo voice or choir, and many are based on Canadian folk songs.

DIACK, J. Michael (1869-1946). Britain. Born in Scotland, Diack lived much of his life in London where he was the head of a publishing company. In addition to this, he was a leading voice teacher and wrote several books on vocal technique. He also edited many choral works by Bach and Händel.

DUNHILL, Thomas Frederick (1877-1946). Britain. Dunhill grew up in London and received his musical training at the Royal College of Music, where he studied composition with Sir Charles Stanford. As a young man, Dunhill served as the assistant music master at the famous boys' school, Eton College. He later taught at the Royal College of Music in London and spent more of his time composing. He wrote some chamber music, two light operas and two ballets. He wrote charming songs, many of them for children, as well as several children's cantatas, operettas, and other works intended for educational purposes.

*FIELDER, Steven (born 1950). Born and  raised in Toronto, Ontario, Fielder graduated from the University of Waterloo and The University of Western Ontario. He currently maintains an active teaching studio at Conservatory Canada (London, Ontario) and also serves as an examiner for piano and theory. Fielder is the author of *Keyboard Harmony & Transposition*, as well as Conservatory Canada's Theory textbooks for Grades 1 to 4.

*FLEMING, Robert (1921-1976). Canada.  Fleming was a composer, pianist, organist, choirmaster and teacher who was born in Prince Albert, Saskatchewan, but moved with his family to Saskatoon when he was 8. His first music lessons were with his mother, but he later studied in England with Arthur Benjamin and Herbert Howells, and in Toronto with Healey Willan. For much of his professional life he was the music director for the National Film Board. He wrote ballets, 250 film scores, works for orchestra and band, 25 chamber works, piano and organ pieces, choral music, hymns, carols and songs. He moved to Ottawa in 1970 where he worked as a teacher and church musician until his death.

FRANZ, Robert (1815-1892). Germany. Franz was born and raised in Halle, the same town where the great composer Händel was born 130 years before. Opposed to the idea of their son becoming a musician, Franz's parents would not allow him to take music lessons until the age of twenty, at which time he left home to study for two years in Dessau. He returned to Halle to begin his career as a composer, but without much success. Finally,

in 1837, Franz published a set of twelve songs that attracted the attention of Schumann. Schumann shared his enthusiasm with other composers such as Mendelssohn and Liszt, and Franz became quite popular in Halle and elsewhere in Europe. Sadly, at the age of 26 he began to lose his hearing. This was complicated by other disabilities that eventually forced him to give up composing altogether. Although Franz is not considered a great composer, he did compose about 350 songs. These songs, while full of tenderness and delicacy, avoid any hint of things passionate or dramatic.

HÄNDEL, Georg Friedrich (1685-1759). Germany and England. Born in Halle, Händel showed early musical talent, but his parents were greatly opposed to the idea of their son becoming a musician. His father finally allowed Georg to study organ and violin. He lived for several years in Italy before moving to England in 1711. He settled in London and enjoyed a long and successful career as a composer of Italian operas and English oratorios. Several of his opera arias have become popular solos today, but are more often sung in English rather than with the original Italian text. Händel's most famous oratorio is the *Messiah*, which is still very popular today.

HUGHES, Herbert (1882-1937). Northern Ireland. Hughes was born in Belfast and was educated at the Royal College of Music in London. He worked in London as a music critic, composer and folksong collector. He helped found the Irish Folk Song Society, and published numerous Irish folk songs that he had collected and arranged with tasteful piano accompaniments. Hughes also edited the two-volume collection, *Irish Country Songs*. He composed a number of original songs, written in a lighter style, that show a delightful sense of humour.

JENKYNS, Peter Thomas Hewitt (born 1921). Britain. Jenkyns spent most of his career as a lecturer in music education in Luton, England. His compositions are intended almost exclusively for young players and singers.

LONGMIRE, John Basil (born 1902). Britain. Longmire received his musical training at the Royal College of Music in London. He spent his entire career as a school music teacher in England, except for a brief period (1950-54) when he lived in New Zealand. Almost all of his compositions are for young people, and include piano music and many songs for use in schools. When he retired, he moved to the Channel Islands.

MILLER, Anne Stratton. Nothing is known of this composer.

MORLEY, Thomas (1557-1603). Britain. Today, Morley is probably the most popular of all Elizabethan composers, perhaps because his English madrigals and ballets are so cheerful and tuneful. He was a well-respected musician in his own day, serving as organist at St. Paul's Cathedral in London, and as a gentleman of the Chapel Royal. Such was his importance that Queen Elizabeth II gave him a monopoly on music printing. In 1597, Morley published his *Plaine and Easie Introduction to Practicall Musicke,* a book on music theory and musical life in England that remained popular for some 200 years. He also composed church anthems, instrumental music, and ayres for voice and lute.

RATHBONE, George. Nothing is known of this composer. He was probably British.

ROWLEY, Alec (1892-1958). Britain. Rowley was born in London and spent his entire career in that city. He studied at the Royal Academy of Music, winning prizes for both composition and piano. He was a fluent and original writer of songs, chamber music, and works for organ and piano. Much of his piano music is attractive and accessible to the young student.

SHARMAN, Cecil (?-1973). Not much is known about Sharman. A number of his vocal pieces were published in the 1930s and they include the collection *Songs of Arthur.*

SULLIVAN, Arthur Seymour (1842-1900). England. Sullivan was born in London into a musical family; his father was an army bandsman and professor of clarinet at the Royal Military School of Music. As a boy Arthur sang in the Chapel Royal choir, and as a youth he won the Mendelssohn Scholarship. This scholarship enabled him to study at the Royal Academy of Music and the Leipzig Conservatory. He composed orchestral music, oratorios, songs, anthems and hymns, but none of these compositions are exceptional. His lasting fame, however, rests on the unique, fun-filled brand of operettas that he composed between 1875 and 1896 in collaboration with the satirical librettist William Gilbert. These stage works took London by storm when they were introduced, and they remain popular today with hundreds of Gilbert & Sullivan Societies worldwide.

*WATSON HENDERSON, Ruth (born  1932). Canada. Watson Henderson was born in Toronto, Ontario where she studied piano with Alberto Guerrero and composition with Oskar Morawetz. After leaving Toronto, she continued her studies in New York. Watson Henderson worked as a teacher and church musician in Winnipeg, Manitoba and Kitchener, Ontario before returning to Toronto where she now works as a piano accompanist and composer. In 1989, her *Chromatic Partita* for organ was an award winner in the International Competition for Women Composers in Mannheim, Germany. She has also written choral and vocal music, as well as works for the piano.

YOUNG, Stuart (20th century). Nothing is known about this composer.

This page intentionally left blank.

GRADE FOUR – EXAMINATION REQUIREMENTS

Length of the examination: 25 minutes

Examination Fee: Please consult the current examination application form for the schedule of fees.

Co-requisite: None. There is NO written examination co-requisite for the awarding of the Grade 4 Practical Certificate.

NOTE: It is recommended that Mature Beginners take Grade 4 as their first examination.

Candidates are expected to know all of the requirements and regulations for the examination as outlined in the current Conservatory Canada Voice Syllabus. In the event of a discrepancy between the current syllabus and the requirements set out below, the Syllabus must be considered definitive for examination purposes. No allowance can be made for candidates who misread or fail to follow any of the regulations and/or requirements for the examinations.

REQUIREMENTS & MARKING

Requirement	Total Marks
FOUR LIST PIECES	
TWO chosen from List A (Folksongs and all other songs before 1900)	24
TWO chosen from List B (Post 1900)	24
ONE SUPPLEMENTARY PIECE	8
VOCALISES: None required	0
TECHNICAL TESTS	16
SIGHT	
Rhythm Pattern	3
Singing	7
AURAL TESTS	10
VIVA VOCE	8
TOTAL POSSIBLE MARKS	100

NOTE: The examination program must include at least ONE piece by a Canadian composer. The Canadian piece may be chosen from the List Pieces OR as the Supplementary Piece.

PIECES

Candidates are required to perform FOUR PIECES contrasting in key, tempo, genre, era and subject: TWO pieces to be chosen from List A, and TWO pieces to be chosen from List B. Your choices must include four different composers. All pieces must be sung from memory. Pieces may be transposed to suit the compass of the candidate's voice.

SUPPLEMENTARY PIECE

Candidates must be prepared to sing from memory ONE SUPPLEMENTARY PIECE. This piece need not be from the Syllabus list, and may be chosen entirely at the discretion of the teacher and student. It may represent a period or style of piece not already included in the examination program, but which holds special interest for the candidate. You may use suitable pieces from the Broadway and musical theatre, to be performed WITHOUT movement, costume or props. The choice must be within the following guidelines:

1) The equivalent level of difficulty of the piece may be at a higher level, providing it is within the technical and musical grasp of the candidate.

2) Pieces below the equivalent of Grade 3 level are not acceptable.

3) The piece must be suitable for the candidate's voice and age.

4) The piece must be solo voice (with or without piano accompaniment). Vocal duets are not acceptable.

Special approval is not required for the Supplementary Piece. However, poor suitability of choice may be reflected in the mark.

TECHNICAL EXERCISES

Candidates must be prepared to sing any or all of the exercises given below, in the following manner:

i)   Sung to vowels

Ah [a], ay [e], ee [i], oh [o], oo [u]

as requested by the examiner. Though the tonic sol-fa names may be used to learn these exercises, candidates may NOT sing using sol-fa names in the examination.

ii) Sung without accompaniment. A starting pitch will be given by the examiner. Exercises may be transposed from the keys given below into keys suitable to the candidate's voice range. The examiner may give a different starting pitch for each exercise.

iii) Metronome markings should be regarded as *minimum* speeds.

iv) Expression markings are not given for Grade 4 and are NOT required for the examination.

v)   All exercises must be sung in a single breath unless a breath mark is indicated in the score by a comma.

vi) A slur has been used to indicate legato singing. Staccato markings have been used to indicate staccato singing.

SIGHT READING

Candidates are required to perform at sight a) a rhythmic exercise and b) a passage of vocal score as described below. The candidate will be given a brief period to scan the score before beginning to sing. Candidates are not permitted to hum the melody while scanning. Candidates must perform the rhythm section without counting aloud. It is recommended that candidates maintain a steady beat, and avoid the unnecessary repetition caused by attempting to correct errors during the performance.

Before the candidate attempts to sing the vocal passage, the Examiner will play on the piano a I-IV-V-I chord progression (with the leading-note to tonic in the upper part) to establish the key and tonality. NO starting note will be given.

a) Rhythm	b) Vocal Passage

To tap, clap or play on one note (at the candidate's choice) a simple rhythm.
 	
    Length   4 bars
    Time signature   2/4, 3/4, 4/4
    Note values   whole, 1/2, dotted 1/2, 1/4,
                        1/8, & dotted 1/4 followed by 1/8,
                        dotted 1/8 followed by 1/16.
    Rest values   whole, 1/2, 1/4, 1/8
	To sing at sight a simple unaccompanied melody, within a range of one octave (*doh* to *doh*) and within the limits of the great (or grand) staff. Candidates may use either any vowel of their choice or the tonic sol-fa names.
	
	  Majors keys only up to and including
	                          3 sharps and flats
	  Length 4-8 bars
	  Time Signature 2/4, 3/4, 4/4
	  Note values whole, 1/2, dotted 1/2, 1/4, 1/8
	  Rest values whole, 1/2, 1/4
	  Melodic Intervals 2nds, 3rds, 4ths, 5ths
	  Beginning on the tonic note

Example: a) Rhythm

Example: b) Vocal Passage

AURAL TESTS

The candidate will be required:

    i)   at the candidate's choice, to play back OR sing back to any vowel, a short melody of six to eight notes, in 2/4, 3/4 or 4/4 time, based on the first five notes of a major scale, after the Examiner has:
              ✓ named the key [only the major keys of *C, F, G* or *D* will be used]
              ✓ played the 4-note chord on the tonic in broken form
              ✓ played the melody twice

The melody will begin on the tonic note. Following is the approximate level of difficulty:

ii) to identify any of the following intervals after each one has been played once by the Examiner in broken form:

<table>
<tr><td>**ABOVE a given note**</td><td>**BELOW a note**</td></tr>
<tr><td>*major 3rd*</td><td>*perfect 4th*</td></tr>
<tr><td>*minor 3rd*</td><td>*perfect 5th*</td></tr>
<tr><td>*perfect 4th*</td><td>*perfect octave*</td></tr>
<tr><td>*perfect 5th*</td><td></td></tr>
<tr><td>*perfect octave*</td><td></td></tr>
</table>

iii) to identify *major* or *minor* triad chords, solid form, in close, root position only. Each triad chord will be played ONCE by the examiner.

iv) to state whether a short passage in *chorale* style, about 6 to 8 bars in length, is in a *major* or a *minor* key, and whether the final cadence is either *Perfect* (V-I) or *Interrupted/Deceptive* (V-VI).

VIVA VOCE

Candidates must be prepared to give verbal answers to questions on the FOUR List pieces selected for the examination. Candidates must ensure that all teaching notes and other written comments are removed from the score before the examination. The questions will include the following elements:

i) to find and explain all of the signs (including clefs, time signatures, key signatures, accidentals, etc.), articulation markings (legato, staccato, accents, phrase or slur markings, etc.), dynamic and tempo markings, and other musical terms as they may be found in the four selected pieces.

ii) without reference to the score, to give the title, key and composer of the piece.

iii) to explain the meaning of the title of the piece.

iv) to give a few relevant details about the composers represented.

v) with direct reference to the score, to explain briefly simple form and key structures, including any obvious modulations.

vi) to play on the piano any note on a white or black key within two octaves above or below middle C, as requested by the Examiner. Candidates are not required to read this note from score.

vii) to play on the piano a *major* triad (root position only) starting on any white or black note within two octaves above or below middle C, as requested by the examiner. The candidate should also be prepared to transform the same triad into a *minor* triad by lowering the third.

O CANADA

Written in French by Adolphe-Basile Routhier (1839-1920) in Quebec City and first performed there in 1880
to a musical setting by Calixa Lavallée. Translated into English in 1908 by Robert Stanley Wier (1856-1926).
Approved as Canada's national anthem by the Parliament of Canada in 1967 and adopted officially in 1980.

Adolphe-Basile Routhier
English version by Robert Stanley Wier

*Calixa Lavallée
(1842-1891)
arr. D.F. Cook

CONSERVATORY CANADA™

Conservatory Canada conducts voice examinations throughout Canada from the Grade 1 level to the professional Associate Diploma level.

Please direct all examination enquiries to:

Office of the Registrar
Conservatory Canada
45 King Street, Suite 61
London, Ontario, Canada
N6A 1B8

Telephone: 519-433-3147
Toll free in Canada: 1-800-461-5367

Fax: 519-433-7404

Email: officeadmin@conservatorycanada.ca